CRYING OVER SPILLED MILK

Life with food allergies and the ripple effects you want to know

LAUREN SOLTWISCH

Cover photograph and author photograph by Noah Gelfman

Cover design by Armend Meha

Editing by Melissa Hillebrand and Christiane Rodes

ISBN: 978-0-578-58249-8

To my family and friends, I literally wouldn't be alive without your support.

To my parents, for watching over me.

To my brother, for standing by me.

To my husband, for loving all of me.

Table of Contents

Top 10 food-allergy related questions I've been asked..v

Preface vi

1. Let's Not Jump to Conclusions... 1
2. K through 12 5
3. College 13
4. Travel & Travel Prep 18
5. The Talk (Not *That* Talk) 26
6. Managing Food Allergies in the Office.. 30
7. A Milk-Free Sex Life 38
8. Wedding Planning.. 44
9. Navigating Food Labels & Ingredients.. 50
10. Foretelling a Future with Food Allergies 54

Top 10 food-allergy related questions I've been asked

And where you can find their answers in this book

What is a food allergy?   *Preface*

How did you find out about your allergies?   Chapter 1

What do you think about all these special accommodations
being made for kids with food allergies?   Chapter 2

Were you bullied as a kid?   Chapter 2

Have you ever used your allergies to get out of something?   Chapter 2

Are you allowed to take your special food to other
countries?   Chapter 4

How do you use an epinephrine auto-injector? Little
jabs, right?   Chapter 6

If I ate a slice of pizza, could I kiss you?   Chapter 7

Are you short because you couldn't drink milk as a kid?   Chapter 10

Do you want kids? Aren't you worried about them
having food allergies?   Chapter 10

Preface

Why should you read a book
about someone's life with food allergies?

"It's no use crying over spilled milk."

You've likely heard this idiom—it's used to emphasize that there's no point worrying over something you cannot change. So what phrase should someone use when her whole life has been undercut by a looming, life-determining worry of what she has no control over?

I'm talking about my deadly food allergies to milk and tree nuts.

You have no idea who I am. You've never laughed at my jokes. You don't know where I stand on politics. And because you don't know me, you really have no reason to trust me. Why would you? If I were to tell you one drop of milk could put me six feet under, what would your immediate reaction be?

She's probably being dramatic.

Wow, she must really hate milk.

Is she lactose intolerant?

I have this sudden urge to pour milk on her head and see what happens.

When I tell people about my food allergies, most are skeptical, and I don't blame them. We often hear about people's dietary preferences masquerading as restrictions.

"I'm gluten free, but I love breadsticks."

"No, no; I was vegan *last* month."

"I'm allergic to tomatoes, but I can eat them as long as they're on a pizza."

With so many claims that don't add up or flip-flop on the daily, how can we *not* begin to question sincerity? And people tend to embellish! It's our way of contributing something juicy to the conversation. If I had a dime for every time someone told me they know exactly how I feel because they're vegetarian by choice, I sure as hell wouldn't be trying to sell this book. (Tell your friends!)

But really, why am I writing a book on living with food allergies?

There is a ton of content available on the topic: allergy-friendly recipes, medical books, picture books for kids, blogs and podcasts for parents. But what I wish I had growing up was a guide that would better prepare me—and those around me—for all of the major life events that would be impacted by my food allergies.

I'm trying to fill this gap. Ultimately, I want to bridge the food allergy community with the rest of the world through mutual understanding. Depending on who you are, I have two objectives.

I hope readers with food allergies will find support after having an uncomfortable date, suffering from a bad reaction, or just a long day at work explaining their allergies over and over to coworkers and clients. I also hope that today's kids with food allergies, when they're older, will read this and be able to better prepare themselves for life's hurdles, or simply find comfort in knowing someone else has ridden—and survived—the allergy-free struggle bus.

I hope readers without food allergies will see what it's like to play a never-ending, life-threatening game of keep away. If you're a parent of a kid with food allergies, I hope my experiences spark meaningful conversations in your family. Furthermore, many people have food allergies, and that number is growing. Medical procedures to treat anaphylaxis resulting from food allergy increased by 360% between 2007 and 2016, according to Food Allergy Research and Education

(FARE).[1] Wall Street Journal reports that nearly 11% of adults have food allergies. Odds are, if you don't have a food allergy, you will come across someone who does—a coworker or boss, a friend, a love interest. I hope this book helps prepare you for these encounters.

So, if you decide to keep reading, I suppose you have no other choice than to trust me.

Now, what exactly is a food allergy?

A food allergy is a medical condition that affects the immune system. Food allergies are often confused with food intolerances, which do not involve the immune system.

Food allergies are IgE mediated, meaning the immune system produces abnormally large amounts of an antibody called immunoglobulin E (IgE). These IgE antibodies fight the "enemy" food allergens by releasing, among other chemicals, histamines, which trigger the symptoms of an allergic reaction. (Over-the-counter allergy medications, such as Benadryl®, are *anti*-histamines.)

One way to test for food allergies is via a skin prick test (SPT), which typically involves a doctor or nurse using a small plastic probe to prick the skin with a tiny amount of the allergen solution just below the skin's surface. The doctor then evaluates the results based on how the skin reacts. Positive SPT reactions typically result in itchy, red bumps, or hives. For example, I've included a picture of my arm when I got tested for various types of seafood. The bottom right hive showed a positive SPT reaction for codfish, which ended up showing positive on my follow-up test: a blood test.

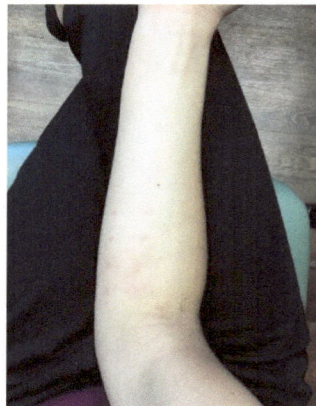

---

[1] FARE is the world's largest non-profit organization dedicated to food allergy awareness, education, research, and advocacy. FARE was founded in 2012, as the result of a merger between Food Allergy & Anaphylaxis Network (FAAN) and the Food Allergy Initiative (FAI). I've turned to this organization for food allergy support and resources throughout my life.

A blood test measures an immune system's response to particular foods by measuring IgEs. I'm including two of my blood test results from 2010 and 2016.

```
                                        Tests Ordered
F002-IgE Milk (Cow); Drawing Fee

        TESTS              RESULT      FLAG      UNITS    REFERENCE INTERVAL   LAB
F002-IgE Milk (Cow)
F002-IgE Milk (Cow)              >100  Abnormal   kJ/L         Class VI        01
Class Description                                                              01
        Levels of Specific IgE      Class  Description of Class
        ----------------------      -----  -------------------
                   <0.05             0         Negative
        0.05  -    0.07             0/I       Equivocal
        0.08  -    0.15             I         Increasing
        0.16  -    0.50             II         levels
        0.51  -    2.50             III          of
        2.51  -   12.50             IV      Specific IgE
       12.51  -   62.50             V        Antibody
       62.51  - >100.00             VI
```
2010

ALLERGEN REPORT

ALLERGY TESTS Performing Lab: CB		CLASS 0 1 2 3 4 5 6	ALLERGY TESTS Performing Lab: CB		CLASS 0 1 2 3 4 5 6
Test Name	Results kU/L		Test Name	Results kU/L	
CASHEW NUT (F202) IGE	9.32 H		TUNA (F40) IGE	0.17 H	
PISTACHIO (F203) IGE	12.00 H		SALMON (F41) IGE	<0.10	
COW'S MILK (F2) IGE	42.50 H		PECAN NUT (F201) IGE	4.93 H	
CODFISH (F3) IGE	3.98 H		WALNUT (F256) IGE	14.80 H	
ALMOND (F20) IGE	5.11 H				
CRAB (F23) IGE	0.76 H				

INTERPRETATION   Performing Lab: CB

See Endnote 1

Endnote 1

```
    Specific                      Level of Allergen
    IGE Class      kU/L           Specific IGE Antibody
    --------       ---------      ---------------------
       0            <0.10         Absent/Undetectable
       0/1         0.10-0.34      Very Low Level
       1           0.35-0.69      Low Level
       2           0.70-3.49      Moderate Level
       3           3.50-17.4      High Level
       4           17.5-49.9      Very High Level
       5            50-100        Very High Level
       6            >100          Very High Level
```
2016

When you read the charts, there is one thing I'd like to point out: Each allergen is assigned a class on a scale of 0 to 6, identifying a range of levels of IgE, expressed via the unit kU/L.

Notice my kU/L results for cow's milk in both the 2010 and 2016 charts. In 2010, my result was in class 6 with over 100 kU/L. (The doctor even circled it. He said he had never seen anyone with IgE levels that high.) In 2016, my results reduced to class 4 with 42.50 kU/L.

Compare that 42.50 kU/L with all the other results in my 2016 chart. Can you spot the next highest kU/L level? Walnut, which gives me an anaphylactic reaction, is in class 3 with 14.80 kU/L. That's a 97% difference from my milk allergy result.

In short, my milk allergy is the real deal.[2]

If you've ever urged someone with food allergies to just try a bite of a certain food and see what happens, please remember these charts. If you were in these shoes, would you risk it?

The third common type of testing for food allergies is an oral food challenge (OFC), where you typically spend the better half of a day in a doctor's office and an allergist orally administers the suspected food in measured doses, increasing throughout the day until you show signs of a reaction. OFCs typically take place after SPTs and/or blood tests to help an allergist come to a definitive diagnosis. In my case, my skin test and my blood test showed positive for codfish, so my allergist did not recommend an OFC.

So, that's the medical speak, but science was never my strong suit. To better help myself understand what was happening to my body when I was having an allergic reaction, I turned it into a story:

STOMACH: What time is it?

EYES: 11:30 a.m.

BRAIN: You can't be hungry, already. You just ate breakfast.

STOMACH: Well, I'm hungry.

UTERUS: Chocolate?

---

[2] While blood test results are not typically used to predict the severity of an allergy, a 2008 study, *Correlation between specific immunoglobulin E levels and the severity of reactions in egg allergic patients*, conducted by the University Hospital of Geneva, Department of Pediatrics, in Geneva, Switzerland, stated, "IgE titres may help to determine the potential risk of a reaction to eggs."

BRAIN: I suppose 11:30 a.m. is an acceptable snack time. Chips?

HANDS: Okay, one sec, you can't find shit in this purse. Ah, here we go.

STOMACH: That's better. You'll all hear from me in about an hour for lunch.

IMMUNE SYSTEM: Wait…what…what is that?!

BRAIN: Calm down; it's nothing. We've eaten these chips before.

TONGUE: Sure, but why am I starting to itch?

BRAIN: I'm sure it's nothing; let it pass.

THROAT: Hey, I'm feeling a little tight.

IMMUNE SYSTEM: I'm calling them.

BRAIN: Now, let's take it easy…they might not be necessary.

EYES: So…I just looked at the ingredients. There's new a disclaimer on this bag of chips: "Manufactured in a facility with milk."

BRAIN: Damn. I wonder if they added a new product or changed manufacturers or if this bag of chips came from a different facility or—

IMMUNE SYSTEM: Bring in the immunoglobulin Es!

BRAIN: Not the IgEs! Everyone, don't you think we're over*reacting*? (Punny, right?) After all, it's just some milk; it's not like it's poisonous to humans.

IGE: Shut up, Brain. We'll handle this intruder…

The ending involves me rushing to open some form of anti-histamine and taking the correct dosage. (By the way, have you ever tried to open those little packets in a rush? It's like they actually want your throat to close.) I gulp ice water. I'm sure there's no medical reason for the water, but I feel the need to drink it to make sure I can still swallow normally.

If this doesn't do the trick, I resort to my epinephrine auto-injector (i.e., Ep-iPen®). Epinephrine, another term for adrenaline, is used to reverse the symptoms of anaphylaxis, a life-threatening reaction.

If I use my EpiPen®, I have to go to the hospital. Why? Sometimes, one injection of epinephrine isn't enough, so it's best to get to a place where they can hook you up. Not to mention the fact that many people with food allergies can experience recurring symptoms, even hours after the first reaction. Best to stay nearby medical professionals.

I'm often asked what happens when I have a reaction. If I touch something I'm allergic to or something that has come into contact with something I'm allergic to (in a sneaky phenomenon called cross contamination), I break out into hives. Half the time I don't even know what I touched or what touched me when I find myself itching my feet, neck, arms, hands, or eyes.

I can handle hives. Anti-histamine pills or creams usually make me feel better. What I'm most afraid of is anaphylaxis, which typically features swelling, hives, lowered blood pressure, dilated blood vessels, trouble breathing, tightness of the throat, nausea, vomiting, fainting, and a feeling of impending doom.

The over-release of my IgEs can actually put me into anaphylactic shock, where my throat closes and, if I'm not properly treated immediately with epinephrine, I will die.

This makes me scratch my head when I consider human evolution. Like, how does this make sense?

> IMMUNE SYSTEM: Don't worry. I took care of it. I attacked that enemy milk with all my IgEs. Now our throat is closing to not let any enemies in ever again! Ha!

> LUNGS: Except now I can't breathe, and we're going to die.

BRAIN: Idiots.

I'm clearly no doctor or scientist. I'm a communications professional who graduated magna cum laude in three-and-a-half years with a major in journalism and a minor in English. All I can offer you is my life story, how my experiences may help you, and why sometimes it's okay to cry over spilled milk.

1
Let's Not Jump to Conclusions

The Don't-Miss Context to the Early Days of My Food Allergies

An epinephrine auto-injector has been within my reach since 1994, so you can imagine my surprise when I first saw one in a TV commercial—in 2012.

I excitedly texted my mom with the news that people with food allergies were finally being recognized, although the advertisement likely ran because the drug manufacturer knew that the number of people with food allergies was rapidly and vastly increasing. (Cha-ching.)

The Centers for Disease Control & Prevention (CDC) reports the prevalence of food allergy in children increased by 50% between 1997 and 2011. As more and more children were developing food allergies, I was doing some developing of my own.

I am my parents' first child. My mom was twenty-six and my dad was twenty-nine when I was born in 1991, which was about the time when they first suspected my allergy to milk. My dad, a commercial airline pilot, was home for a few days before his next trip, taking care of me while my mom was back at work as a nurse after her maternity leave. When my dad reached for the pumped breast milk, he realized they were fresh out.

My dad fed me formula, instead, which contained milk. I immediately spit it up, which babies tend to do. Why would he think anything of it? I ended up rejecting the formula again, and again, so my dad took me to my mom so I could eat.

My mom, who has seen her fair share of medical conditions, suspected a possible milk allergy and took me to a pediatrician. She explained how I rejected multiple formulas multiple times and how milk was the consistent ingredient in the equation.

The doctor said, "Food allergies are extremely rare. Let's not jump to conclusions."

My parents stopped giving me milk and milk products when I was nine months old. When I was three, I was tested for a milk allergy via an OFC, which involved the doctor giving me a cookie containing milk. This was how I was tested for a food allergy in 1994. Let's pause for a moment to appreciate today's diagnostic measures.

As I said, I was three, and all I knew was to do anything, *anything*, but consume milk. I knew I shouldn't have taken that one bite of the cookie when my feet began to itch and burn, which moved up throughout my whole body, chest tightening and throat closing, all the while feeling betrayed and confused.

That day, I was officially diagnosed with a milk allergy and prescribed my first epinephrine auto-injector. What followed were annual visits to an allergist for SPTs to see when I would grow out of it. After all, the odds that I would have a food allergy into adulthood were extremely rare. (I was eighteen years old when my allergist told me I likely would not grow out of my food allergies and no longer needed annual tests.)

When I was six, I found out about my tree nut allergy. I was playing at a neighbor's house when the mom brought out a can of cashews. She read the ingredients and offered for me to read them, too. (At this point, I didn't know half the words I was reading, but I was definitely triggered by "milk," "whey," and "casein.")

There was no sign of milk. I tried a small handful.

My feet immediately began to itch and I couldn't breathe. That's all I remember from that day, but I'm told I was rushed to urgent care.

Can you imagine what my parents must have thought and felt? Before accommodations for food allergies became the norm—or the law—my parents packed my meals every day, spent an extra thirty minutes at the grocery store reading ingredients and nutrition labels, called parents ahead of birthday parties and teachers ahead of field trips to ensure I only ate what my parents packed and to double check that my EpiPen® was within reach. They would bake cakes and make pizzas from scratch. They labeled anything in our house containing milk or tree nuts with an "X" to let me know it wasn't safe. They drew the letter "L" on the caps of my water bottles so other people would know not to drink out of them because they could have eaten something I was allergic to. Quite frankly, I'm exhausted just typing this paragraph.

My brother, Matthew, was born three years after me in 1994. As a child, he was never trusted to pour his own glass of milk. All he wanted was some "milk in a bowl" (his way of asking for cereal with milk, opposed to dry cereal).

We had separate bowls and utensils and placemats—mine were red, his blue. My chore was to unload the clean dishes; his was to load the dirty dishes. He would wipe down the counters; I would sweep the floors.

On Halloween (my trick-or-treating years were way before FARE's Teal Pumpkin Project®), Matthew and I would dump our candy bags in separate piles in the living room and practice our trading skills. He only wanted chocolate, and I only wanted the milk- and nut-free candy.

"You want to give me *one* pack of Skittles® for my Reese's™? Make it *two* packs and you've got a deal," I'd bargain.

When several families would get together to play cards and the kids would play in the basement, Matthew helped me keep watch for which video game controller was touched by a kid who just ate cheddar popcorn. When his friends came to our

3

house, he made them wash their hands immediately after they ate ice cream. He was painfully and acutely aware that one wrong move could cost his sister's life.

Imagine how Matthew felt when I once accidentally took a sip from his blue sippy cup. Okay, "accidentally" is the wrong word. I knew my kitchen utensils were red, but his blue sippy cup was usually filled with juice. I *loved* juice, and I already had my allotted quantity for the day.

I tipped back the blue sippy cup and saw a white, creamy liquid appear through the opaque lid. My face turned as white as the milk I just drank. My parents were having a dinner party at the time. You can probably picture the looks on their faces when I walked into the dining room and declared that I drank milk from Matthew's blue sippy cup. (After all their color-coding efforts, nonetheless!)

In 2010, when I left our home in Cincinnati for college in Chicago, it was the beginning of a new era for my parents and brother. They could order out! They could leave a mess in the kitchen! Matthew could pour his own milk! (Just kidding, he was sixteen and developed his fine motor skills by this point.) My family joked that they would be the ones to gain the "freshman fifteen" from eating the foods they kept out of the house for nineteen years.

It was a new era for me, too. I was about to test my independence and be a grown-up without feeling my family's eyes on me with every bite.

When my parents dropped me at the dorms, my mom said with a smile and a tear in her eye, "Lauren, we've kept you alive to see nineteen; don't go messing up all those years of hard work, okay?"

I laughed and said, "Let's not jump to conclusions."

2
K through 12

The Formative Years That Set the Foundation for How I Socially Handle My Food Allergies

I don't think children fully comprehend what it means to have food allergies, other than there is certain food to never be touched or eaten. Then, they're at school for a good portion of the day, out of their parents' sight, surrounded by curious classmates and busy teachers. There's a fine line between curiosity, bullying, or an accidental bite of the class snack and a trip to the emergency room, or even death.

FARE reports about 40% of children with food allergies experience a severe reaction, such as anaphylaxis, and childhood hospitalizations for food allergies tripled between the late '90s and the mid-2000s. It's terrifying for parents to wonder, on an hourly basis, if their child is surviving. That's a lot of trust to have in others—often complete strangers—tasked with caring for many children at once.

Today, there are roughly two kids with food allergies in every classroom, FARE estimates. When I attended grade school in the mid-'90s, I was one of two students with food allergies in the entire school. Schools have changed drastically in the past three decades for students with food allergies. There are allergen-free lunch tables, labeled lunch menus, support groups, and education and training exercises; the CDC even published *Voluntary Guidelines for Managing Food Allergies in Schools and Early Care and Education Programs* in 2013.

My parents had to pave their own way on my road to safety at school. They decided to meet with my grade school principal, Mr. B, to discuss their concerns. They wanted to volunteer their time to help raise food allergy awareness. They asked for parent chaperones to be trained on using my EpiPen®. They wanted me off lunch-table-cleaning duty. (Cafeteria tables have all sorts of crumbs and spills and I was in no position to come into contact with them, and everyone ate in communal spaces; there were no allergen-free tables.)

During birthday parties, which involved cake in the classroom comprising about fifteen students and one teacher, they asked for either a rule for kids to wash their hands after eating cake, or to omit cake from the classroom entirely. The cake broke the camel's back, so the story goes.

Mr. B asked, "Why would I sacrifice other kids' happiness for just one kid?"

Ouch.

Mr. B's "greater good" response stings, but I'll play devil's advocate; he wasn't necessarily wrong. However, mentalities like Mr. B's at such an early stage of my life are at the root of my social anxiety.

I remember the looks on some parents' faces that seemed to say, *Lauren's going to be at the party; does this mean my kid won't get cake? She should have just not been invited.*

I remember wondering if my presence alone directly correlated to other kids' unhappiness, and I felt like I was a constant burden to my classmates, my teacher, my parents, my brother.

That's a lot on a six-year-old's shoulders.

Before I reveal the outcome of Mr. B's response, it's important to have a basic understanding of the Americans with Disabilities Act (ADA) of 1990. It's a civil rights law that prohibits discrimination against individuals with disabilities in all areas of public life, including jobs, schools, transportation, and all public and private places that are open to the general public.

Under the ADA, a disability is defined as a physical or mental impairment that substantially limits one or more major life activities of an individual. Among these major life activities are eating and breathing. As severe allergic reactions typically affect your heart, circulatory system, digestive system, and breathing and respiratory systems, the ADA recognizes a food allergy as a disability.

Back to Mr. B. One of my parents' friends (and the mother of one of my class-mates) was on the school board. After hearing of Mr. B's refusal to make any food allergy accommodations in his school, she approached him and explained that he's looking at an ADA lawsuit if he doesn't get on the same page. Only then did he change his mind. (My parents waited until I was an adult to tell me this story, then it became clear why Mr. B shot me dirty looks when I was in first grade.)

I have a theory to explain why people have thoughts like: *Why does my kid have to sacrifice a peanut butter sandwich at lunch for some other kid?*

It fundamentally has to deal with the fact that accommodations for every other disability—whether someone is in a wheelchair, hearing impaired, blind, or re-quires a different approach to learning—do not directly inconvenience other peo-ple. If there's a ramp, others can still walk on that. If there's a sign language inter-preter in the room, others can still listen. If there's Braille on a bathroom door sign, others can still identify a bathroom. If a student requires specialized educa-tion, others can still pursue the traditional curriculum.

But accommodating for food allergies can unfortunately require others to make momentary dietary sacrifices, and this pisses people off.

How was I going to make friends? I had seen TV shows where the kid with food allergies was portrayed as a nerd, bullied, and an outcast, and I was not about to subscribe to that persona.

I have always felt awkward in social situations, and I used to wonder if I could thank my food allergies for that. The more I thought about it, the more I realized eating is the anchor of most social situations. Even the Latin roots for "compan-ion" break down to com-, meaning "with," and panis, meaning "bread" or "food." Food is a building block of friendship. When you can't exactly partake in food-related activities, things get awkward.

Take eating out, for example. If I eat at a restaurant and explain my food aller-gies to the server, I risk appearing high-maintenance or getting sick. Both are un-comfortable situations for everyone involved.

If I bring my own food to a restaurant, I feel the need to act like it's the best damn thing I've ever tasted when people look at me pitifully and ask if I'm enjoying my turkey sandwich I made six hours earlier. And that's assuming the restaurant allows me to eat my own food. One restaurant manager told me to eat my sandwich outside or put it in my purse until we left. Needless to say, it killed the mood.

If I don't eat at all, which is what I normally do, this is where things get really awkward. Imagine you're having a meal with me in a small group. While you eat, I try to balance the amount of time I talk with how much I stare at you while you chew your food. To avoid awkward silences, I try to keep the conversation going, so I strategically notice when you take a break from your plate to ask you a question. (I actually had a teammate in college who refused to sit at my table because she felt so guilty and awkward eating in front of me.) I excuse myself to go to the bathroom, and this is likely when you can relax. Finally, when the bill comes and everyone wants to split it evenly, I look like a cheapskate when I say I'm only paying for my drink.

Am I awkward because of my food allergies? Absolutely.

How was I going to make friends in grade school? I had an idea.

I'd give my share of the class snack or treat to my classmates! Before I knew it, kids lined up to my desk to make their case on why they should get my Halloween cookie. Some of those kids started to come over just to talk to me, which grew into very special friendships (and they say you can't buy friends).

I carried over this food-sharing, friend-making tactic into high school, where word got out that I was giving away treats, and students from other cafeteria tables would come over to mine and ask for my Valentine's Day cupcake. (No matter your age, if you have food allergies, I highly recommend using this as a way to strike up conversations with strangers—who doesn't like free food? Besides people with food allergies…)

In high school, I was a little wiser and could taste independence, but was not used to this new autonomy. From packing my own lunch to driving myself to school to participating in extra-curricular activities (like playing volleyball and founding and managing the school's writing center), I felt very self-empowered and grown-up. I could, for the first time, begin to make my own decisions and take control of my life with food allergies. And that meant I would be faced with new, *er*, learning opportunities.

For instance, in geometry class, my close friend, Annie (who remains one of my closest friends today), gave me a stick of gum. About two chews in, my throat felt tight. Trying not to make a scene, I asked her for the pack. Her eyes widened; she knew what this meant. She handed it to me and, to my dismay, the ingredients contained milk. I quietly excused myself and headed toward the door. The teacher asked where I was going.

Annie exclaimed, "I gave her gum with milk in it and I think I killed her!"

(If I wouldn't allow myself to come across as dramatic, I sure surrounded myself with friends who would establish urgency on my behalf.)

The teacher told me to run to the nurse's office and told Annie to run with me.

I was lucky to have the kindest school nurse on the planet. When Annie and I ran into her office, she instinctively reached for a pack of Benadryl® and my prescribed EpiPen®. (I was not allowed to carry it on my person.)

Two pink pills and about ten minutes later, I was breathing normally again. The nurse told me to drive home before I became too drowsy, and she called my mom to let her know what happened. On my drive, my mom called me from work. I told her I was fine and I'd see her at home, where I'd likely be sleeping. I went back to school the next day, and all was well.

One of the questions I've been asked is if I've ever used my allergies to get out of something. I wish I could deny this, but there was one time.

I had a math test I was definitely not prepared for. In fact, I had totally forgotten there was a test until a classmate asked for my study guide at the lockers.

The memory of me being immediately sent home after the chewing gum incident flashed through my mind. I quickly dismissed it. I was not about to fake an allergic reaction as an excuse to delay a test—I know the story about the boy who cried wolf. I put myself in solitude in the library with my eight-pound math book and the study guide I denied to my classmate.

It became very apparent very quickly that I could not possibly learn the material in time. I weighed my options: I could fail the test, or I could lie about an allergic reaction and be sent home. I was not a fan of either of those options, but when you attend a private, Catholic, college-preparatory school for girls, failing is simply not an option. All I wanted was more time to study, really. What was the harm in one little white lie?

I regrettably went to the nurse and told her I wasn't feeling well, and it may have been something I ate. The nurse had me call my mom, who said she'd meet me at home. I told her to stay at work because I just needed to sleep. I lied, worried the nurse, and caused my mom stress, but I studied—and still barely passed the test. Lying about that allergic reaction haunts my memory more than failing that test would have.

Another question I'm often asked is if I was ever bullied due to my food allergies. There were a handful of times where students would accidentally flip their spoon of ice cream onto my arm, but I never felt like I was being targeted because of my inability to consume milk or tree nuts. There are only two instances I can remember that may have crossed the line.

My freshman year of high school, I was sitting at a lunch table before class, and a girl asked about my food allergies. I pointed out that if her cheese puff touched me, I would break out into hives. She thought I was exaggerating.

I was desperate to prove it, eager to not establish my reputation as being dramatic or dishonest. So, I told her to rub the cheese puff on my leg. Guess what? She did. You know where this is going—I broke out into hives. I went to the nurse to get Benadryl®, and a rumor started that I was rushed to the hospital. I returned to school the next day, and the girl apologized with flowers.

The other time was at a family dinner. I was twelve years old, and we were meeting my step-cousins for the first time. I was at the kids' table. The younger of my new cousins crinkled his nose and asked about my milk allergy. I, trying to put it into terms a six-year-old would understand, told him that if the milk in the glass in front of him touched me, I would get red and itchy bumps on my skin.

He took a moment to ponder this, looked at his glass of milk, and, in one swift motion, poured the entire glass of milk over my head. I just sat there, in a bit of a shock.

My poor brother, who up until this point had spent his nearly ten years on Earth trying to avoid this exact situation, yelled for the adults. My mom scrubbed me down in the shower while my aunt ran to the trunk of her car to get her workout clothes for me to wear the rest of the evening.

My cousin may not share my sentiment, but I laugh whenever I visit this memory. I love my cousin; he's a brilliant artist without a mean bone in his body. He inspired the cover idea for this book! I'd say we're even. And I'll never forget when he showed up to my volleyball tournament the next day and gave me flowers and a card you can't find at a Hallmark store.

"I'm sorry I poured milk on your head. I didn't know you would get red and itchy bumps," was hand-written next to crayon-drawn stick figures of us holding hands, and a big, red "X" was scribbled over the outline of a glass of milk.

Was I ever bullied in the way kids are mean to other kids? Not in my opinion. I'd actually say it was the adults who acted more like bullies than the kids.

In fact, I recently saw a social media post where a food allergy mom asked how to handle this situation: A family with a child with food allergies brought a peanut-butter sandwich to an event, and they sat nearby her son, who has a severe food allergy of his own—to peanuts. When asked to move, the family got offended and abruptly left the event. Put yourself in the kids' shoes and they likely saw their parents fighting over whose allergy was worse. I bet you can play out the ripple effects in your imagination.

If I could offer advice to anyone who's ever grumbled over food allergy accommodations, I'd encourage them to try to remember a food allergy is no one's fault, safety precautions are not meant to make other lives miserable, and the slightest sign of annoyance can make a significantly negative impact on the self-esteem, self-worth, and sense of belonging of someone with food allergies.

3
College

Holy Shit, Where's My Mom?

I was a junior in high school and had just been recruited to play volleyball at a small, private college just outside the city limits of Chicago. I was on top of the world. I dreamed of all the adventures I'd have. And I wondered how I would handle my food allergies on my own.

Before I even left home, negotiating the terms of my college residence was no easy feat. I was hoping to get my own place with a kitchen where I could prepare my own meals. I did not want to live with strangers who did not understand my food allergies. I did not want to live in a small space where macaroni and cheese in the microwave would cause the allergen to be airborne and affect my ability to breathe.

However, I quickly learned that, as a student-athlete, I needed to stay on campus my freshman year, with at least one roommate. I also learned that I could not opt out of the meal plan. Well, I was not about to spend thousands of dollars on food I had no intention of eating.

I had to get a doctor's note verifying the severity of my food allergies, on which the allergist added that I should occupy a single dormitory room and I will not be able to safely eat from the cafeteria's menu.

I ended up getting my own room and, instead of buying the meal plan, I purchased a pre-paid card intended for things like labeled snacks and beverages available for purchase on campus. In my room, I kept a microwave and the largest-possible-sized refrigerator that was allowed in the dorms (well, maybe a smidge over the limit).

When doing the typical college dorm shopping, my mom and I had a few additions to the standard list. Sheets? Check. Shower caddy? Check. Utensils? Pots and pans? Dish soap and sponges? Mini egg cooker? Check, check, check, check. We also packed my bicycle and a new basket for it, so that I could bike to the nearby grocery store to get my food for the week.

Buying my own groceries took some time to figure out. After one of my first trips, I bought too many groceries for my bike and basket to handle. Bags were in my backpack and basket, two bags hung from each handlebar, and two more bags slumped on the ground next to me. I called one of my teammates, Becca, who drove me and my groceries back to campus. She is a dear friend to this day. (And that's not just because she was the only one I knew with a car on campus.)

You'd think cooking with these fresh ingredients and playing NCAA volleyball would make me fit as a fiddle. You'd *think* that.

I was soon overwhelmed with two-a-day practices, coursework, and taking the time to prepare my own meals. Something had to give, and it wasn't going to be volleyball or my grades. My many bags of fresh meat and veggies turned into a few bags of microwave meals and snacks. While my teammates, friends, and classmates ate in the dining hall, I hurried to my dorm room to scarf down meals between practices and classes. I'd often snack late at night while I was studying or working on projects. I started to gain weight, but wrote it off as the "freshman fifteen."

I knew my diet and eating habits became a problem when my volleyball coach called me into her office, sat me down, and said, "I'd like to talk to you about your weight."

"Waht 'bout iht?" I said, face stuffed with a peanut butter Oreo®. (Not really, but peanut butter Oreos® were a primary culprit. Which is crazy, right? Oreos® are, after all, Milk's Favorite Cookie™, but miraculously have no milk or milk products in the ingredients. And in case you were wondering: Peanuts are not tree nuts; they grow from the ground.)

My coach took me to see the athletic trainer, where we measured my weight. I had gained thirty pounds from August to December. Thirty pounds! When I went home for Christmas, I floored my family.

"And we said *we'd* be the ones to gain the 'freshman fifteen,'" my mom joked.

I ended up taking my car from home to college to make transporting groceries easier. A few of my teammates were majoring in nutrition, and they helped me plan my meals and explained some basic causes of weight gain, like eating late at night.

I lost the weight within the next few months, but that didn't mean my food allergy struggles were over. Remember when my mom told me not to mess up nineteen years of my parents' hard work, and I laughed and told her not to jump to conclusions? I was about to experience karma at its finest.

Being independent in high school was one thing, but living on my own in a different time zone than my parents was a whole new level. When I'd go out to eat and look at a menu, I wouldn't feel my parents' nervous stares. If I wanted to try to order, my mom and dad wouldn't be across the table, shaking their heads. There would be no big fights that ended with me pouting the rest of the evening, woefully sipping my soda and looking enviously at everyone's plates. I was more than ready to break free of those chains and test my ability to handle my food allergies all on my own.

My freshman year, the team traveled to Boston for a tournament. One night, we all went to a restaurant for dinner; we had to play early the next day. The restaurant had this really neat touch-screen kiosk where you could look up menu items based on your allergen. I had never seen anything like this before.

If they have this option, they must take food allergies seriously, I remember thinking.

With my pointer finger, I tapped my way to a list of milk- and nut-free plates. I chose a basic pasta dish; it looked like the safest option.

My assistant coach, who also has professional culinary experience, spoke to the chef directly about my food allergies, explaining that cross contamination was a big issue. The chef assured me and my assistant coach that my dish would be safe.

When everyone's plates made their way to the table, I took one small bite of my pasta. This was my normal practice when trying anything new; if I was heading toward an anaphylactic reaction, I would be able to tell almost instantly.

Minutes passed. I felt fine. I took another bite and waited a few more minutes, just to be safe. I was, after all, in a new city with a new team and didn't want to embarrass myself. I was able to finish the bowl and I was ecstatic.

See, mom and dad? I can eat out with no issues.

In the van on the way back to the hotel, I started to feel, well, off. I didn't think I was having a reaction because my tongue or throat didn't itch. My stomach turned. I tried to stay calm and quiet; it could have been just my anxiety. When we got back to the room, I felt worse. My whole body itched. I wheezed. I took a few Benadryl® pills, then ran to the bathroom, where those pills came right back up.

I continued this cycle for hours. My coach wanted to call 911, but I wouldn't allow it. I had my EpiPen® at the ready, but I knew that if I used it, I would need to visit the emergency room—and worse, my parents would find out I did the one thing they told me not to do.

My teammates let me have the bed closest to the bathroom and all to myself. They were supportive and understanding. The next morning, my coach didn't let me play, but I don't blame her for that decision. She knew as well as I did that allergic reactions can come back hours after the fact, and there was no way I'd be able to perform well with the night I had.

I was humiliated and angry with myself. I called my close friend, Mollie, when we got back to Chicago to tell her what happened and seek emotional support. I begged her not to tell my parents. She swore she wouldn't. When I went home to watch one of my brother's football games that fall, Mollie's mom came up to me and my parents sitting in the bleachers.

"Lauren, how are you feeling since Boston?" she asked with sincerity.

My parents looked at her, then at me, then back at her.

"I told Mollie not to tell...*my parents*," I said. Damn syntax.

This unfortunate experience didn't stop me from trying to eat out at trusted restaurants—although I'd only order a plain salad, and by that I mean a bowl of lettuce—but it did teach me more about my limits, that all my reactions would not be the same, the importance of my support system, and to never be afraid to use my EpiPen® and get proper medical attention at the risk of my parents finding out.

As I progressed through my remaining years as an undergraduate, I became more comfortable managing my food allergies on my own.

My sophomore year, I lived in a cluster of dorm rooms with a common kitchen, sharing the space with my teammates, but there were a few instances where cheesy nachos fell on my bed, or steaming hot chocolate made me wheeze. By the time I was a junior, I yearned for my personal space again, so I went back to a single room until I graduated.

It required practice and the support of my coaches, teammates, friends, and parents, but when it came to attending college with food allergies, I learned to balance the scales—without breaking one.

4
Travel & Travel Prep

Leaving the Comfort of My Own Kitchen

When writing this book, I'd often sit down with a glass of wine, play some music, pull out my laptop, and let out a short, baffled laugh. Because, statistically speaking, I shouldn't even be alive. It would be one thing if I were a hermit who bought the same groceries week after week and used my own kitchen and my own utensils day after day—if I secluded myself from any potential harm. But, between playing travel volleyball and traveling often with my family (remember, my dad is a pilot), there were millions of chances for me to have a life-threatening reaction.

I played travel volleyball for fourteen years, from age eight to twenty-two. I have memories of teammates throwing buttered popcorn around during breaks, hives appearing on my hands and arms after touching the ball, and eating peanut-butter sandwiches in bathroom stalls.

Back then, you were not, under any circumstances, allowed to bring outside food into tournaments. Oh, no. You were going to eat their greasy pizza, fries, slushies, candy, and popcorn, and you were going to perform at your highest level.

I was usually sneaky about bringing in my own food. (Who wanted to search through a sweaty volleyball bag?) Only a handful of times did the tournament directors scold me. When they did, all I had to do was show them my EpiPen® and say I can't eat the options from the concession stand because I have food allergies. If they pushed back, my mom was at the ready to ask them where the ambulance could park after I tried to eat their food. And that was that.

Of course, most travel experiences aren't confined to gymnasiums. Think of somewhere you've vacationed recently. What did you do? Go sightseeing? Taste the local cuisine?

Comedian Jim Gaffigan gives my favorite summary of a vacation when he says:

"Really, that's all a vacation is: Just us eating in a place we've never been. 'Well, why don't we eat something, then we'll go and get something to eat? Then we'll see that thing we're supposed to see…they probably got a snack bar there, right? After that, we should probably get something to eat, though. Then we'll eat somethin'.'"

People with food allergies are probably the only people who actually lose weight on vacations, but before you go calling us the lucky ones, imagine this: You're prepping for a week-long beach vacation and you're packing your sun hat, a book, sunglasses, outfits, shoes, etc., as well as planning and packing for breakfast, lunch, and dinner every day—that's twenty-one meals!

Sounds daunting, right? But, it can be done.

I learned all my tricks from my parents. My dad brought his pilot experience to the table, and my mom brought her attention to detail. From camping and spending days on the lake to going on road trips and flying across the country, I had nearly every type of travel experience under my belt. I watched my parents meet with the head chef on our Hawaii vacation to discuss how I could safely eat at the resort-wide pig roast. I watched my mom meticulously pack coolers before road trips. I watched and my dad make lists of grocery stores near our final destinations' airports (he has been to almost every airport and every airport hotel in the U.S.). By the time I first traveled via plane by myself, I wasn't afraid of flying, like most first-time fliers—I was afraid I didn't pack enough food.

Years later, my husband and I attended a destination wedding in Punta Cana in April 2019. My typical approach to eating at weddings was to consume a heavy meal at home beforehand and pack a snack in my clutch. Attending a wedding in another country, and staying in that country for just under a week, without my parents, would be a new experience for me.

I strategically packed before our flight. My carry-on bag was full of clothes, non-perishable snacks, and several peanut-butter sandwiches. My personal item contained my wallet, a few snacks, and one turkey sandwich. I tend to pack peanut-butter sandwiches because they travel well, fill me up, and don't perish as quickly as turkey sandwiches; however, when I plan for my in-flight meals, I choose the turkey sandwich and keep my peanut-butter sandwiches packed away in case a fellow passenger has a severe peanut allergy. (See the strategy at work?)

My checked bag was full of my food for the week (bananas, microwavable soups, bread, peanut butter, and other snacks). If my checked bag got lost, I'd at least have a sandwich every day, and I could survive on that. When I travel, I'm accustomed to eating not for enjoyment, but for survival.

There is a lot to think about, but I never let my food allergies get in the way of my final destination. If I can do it, you can, too. The following pages contain checklists I use when prepping for travel. (Feel free to rip them out or make copies to use on your own!)

Booking flights:

☐ **Look up the airline's policy on food allergies.** Certain airlines will not allow you to take any precautions prior to boarding your flight, such as cleaning the seat, and they may also serve snacks, like cheese crackers or peanuts, despite any requests not to. (On that note, I can't help but laugh when a gate agent welcomes those with disabilities to board first, yet someone with a food allergy—a disability—can't board with this group to wipe down their seat.)

For additional context, here is a section of one airline's policy on nut allergies: "We can't accommodate requests to not serve certain foods or to provide nut 'buffer zones.' Our planes are cleaned regularly, but can't guarantee the removal of nut allergens on surfaces or in the air filters..."

☐ **Learn what food items are permitted by the Transportation Security Administration (TSA).** The TSA website has an entire section on food, listing what type of food and in what quantities are allowed in your checked bag, carry-on bag, or no bag.

☐ **If traveling internationally, check what food items are allowed through that country's customs and border protection.** When my family was flying from the U.S. to the Bahamas, we got stopped for having sealed lunch meat in our bag, though I don't know if this experience would hold true today. Always check ahead of your flight.

Booking accommodations:

☐ **Find a place with a kitchen or kitchenette, or at least a fridge and microwave.** If you're staying in a hotel, you can usually call ahead of time to ensure a mini-fridge and microwave are in your room. If you find a place with a kitchen, wash every household utensil before use, or you may want to bring your own pans, bowls, utensils, etc. But again, be careful of what you check versus put in your carry-on. I once packed a butter knife in my carry-on bag so I could spread peanut butter on my bagels— TSA did not like that.

☐ **Look up a nearby place to buy groceries.** Even if you're the type to over-pack, there's a good chance you'll forget something, or someone else will eat your food by mistake thinking it's communal.

☐ **Research nearby food-allergy-friendly restaurants.** If you have food allergies but are still comfortable eating out, come up with a list of restaurants ahead of time. Apps like Spokin or AllergyEats are designed to help you navigate allergy-friendly restaurants and other accommodations.

Packing your bag:

In addition to all your clothes and toiletries, pack:

☐ At least two epinephrine dispensers and enough antihistamines as if you were planning on having a reaction each day.

☐ A piece of paper or notecard that says what you are allergic to, including any medicine, as well as any medication you're currently taking, and your emergency contact's full name and phone number. If traveling internationally, make another copy translated into that country's primary language. (I keep my notecard in my wallet next to my ID.)

☐ A copy of your health insurance card.

☐ Snacks and meals. In your carry-on bag, pack simple, TSA-approved food (i.e., sandwiches, baggies of carrots, etc.). In your checked bag, pack any food that isn't allowed in a carry-on bag (i.e., microwaveable bowls of soup, jars of peanut butter…knives…).

☐ Stickers or a marker to mark your food items so they don't get mistaken for food for all, if you're traveling with a group.

Loading the car for a road trip:

☐ **Pack a tote or lunchbox full of "easy-access" snacks to keep near your seat.** If your group goes through the drive-thru, you probably don't want to deal with parking the car, opening the trunk, and digging through bags and coolers to find your food.

☐ **Pack a larger cooler full of your perishable food to keep in the trunk.** This will save you a trip to the grocery store, and your piggy bank will thank you. If you're taking a long road trip and will need more ice, you can buy it when you stop for gas.

☐ **Mark your food with stickers or a marker, or keep your food in designated, separate bags.** If you're traveling somewhere with a group—let's say for spring break—your snacks are going to get eaten (lookin' at you, Becca). You're going to be hangry until you're able to stop at a gas station or grocery store.

Tip for those without food allergies but traveling alongside someone with food allergies: Be patient and don't eat our food. Don't even ask. We already feel like an inconvenience because we need to stop at the grocery store when everyone just wants to get to the beach. Don't make us take a second trip because you ate our food.

Sometimes, the hardest part of traveling with food allergies has nothing to do with packing, but constantly putting on a happy face at the dinner table or convincing others that they should not worry about me and enjoy their vacation.

When traveling with my family, there would be friction. Despite being in my early twenties, my mom or dad would still come over to me in the kitchen of our vacation home and ask if I cleaned the pan first before using it. I felt like a child. I'd usually make a passive-aggressive comment that it's a miracle I survive on my own in Chicago, then they'd remind me of that time in Boston.

I was and will always be my parents' little girl, but it was time I established boundaries. This sounds more mature than what really happened. All of these emotions came pouring out on one family vacation, a turning point for me and my family and my food allergies, which calls for a chapter of its own.

5
The Talk (Not *That* Talk)

The Grown-Up Conversation for
When Kids with Food Allergies Grow Up

When you're a kid with food allergies and aren't growing out of them, you're forced to grow up with them. You'll have conversations with family members and friends that can be uncomfortable, but will help you feel less like a sheltered, helpless child and more like a responsible, independent grown-up.

I am grateful for my upbringing. My family and friends have supported me every step of the way. That doesn't mean everything has been sunshine and rainbows when it comes to these relationships. I've snapped at friends for eating my food (sorry, Becca!), and I've pouted at my parents for, well, a lot of things.

They'd ask to read the ingredients after I read them to make sure I didn't miss anything. They'd watch me like a hawk when I pulled out a cooking utensil to make sure I washed it first. They'd eye me from across the table when I looked at the menu, even if I was only looking to feel included. Whenever someone would ask about my food allergies, I would get about two or three words out before my parents jumped in to answer for me.

My parents and I stumbled through this dance for most of my teenage years and young adulthood. Every time we got together and food was involved, there was this dark bubble I felt hovering over me. It popped on one family vacation.

I brought my then-boyfriend, now-husband, on the trip. A few days passed without confrontation between me and my parents. We were in an isolated cottage in the mountains (which we booked after confirming the location of the nearest hospital—thirty minutes away).

I was making myself dinner before the rest of the family took over the kitchen to make theirs. I could sense people were hungry and I was on the clock. I was about to make pasta. I checked the ingredients on the dish soap (even though I had checked it already in the grocery store with my mom), pulled out the pot and washed it with a clean paper towel. (I feel so wasteful doing this, but reusable sponges are a common cause of cross contamination.)

I glanced up; my mom was talking with her sister and my dad was nowhere in the room. With another clean paper towel, I dried the pot and filled it with water to boil. I crossed the kitchen to grab the pasta box from the cabinet designated for my food. When I turned around, my dad was standing between me and the stove. He asked if I had washed the pot. What happened next I am not exactly proud of.

I know in my heart that everything my parents say or do comes from a place of love. But in this moment, I had let so much frustration build up that I let it all out like a fire-breathing dragon.

"Did you wash that?" my dad asked.

"For the thousandth time, yes, dad."

"I only asked once."

"Once *this evening*."

My mom looked at me with a warning in her eyes. I had enough.

"You both have no idea what I go through on an hour-to-hour basis. Did you even know that I was feeling pressure to hurry up and cook my dinner so you all can eat?"

"No one was rushing you," my mom said.

"No one had to! I can tell people are hungry and I can tell I'm the one thing standing between them and the golden keys to the kitchen. I am so sick of you two treating me like I'm still six years old! It's a miracle I live on my own in Chicago, I know. How can Lauren possibly take care of herself? You have no idea, so stop acting like you do!"

I took my first breath since my dad asked about the pot. I then locked eyes with my husband-to-be in the background. His eyes contained kindness, understanding, and forgiveness. I shifted my stare back to my parents' eyes. Theirs contained anger, surprise, and hurt. I began to cry and left the room.

When things calmed down, my parents and I had a very mature conversation about boundaries and cooperation. They said they'd stop pestering me with questions and I promised I'd cut them some slack.

I wish I had taken the initiative long before that moment to have an adult conversation, instead of throwing a fit like a child demanding to be treated like an adult.

I follow a lot of food allergy parents on social media, and I see the extremely selfless and loving things these parents do. I see their frustration when they try to understand what they possibly could have done to prevent their children from having food allergies. I see how protective they are. I see how deeply they care.

That said, I can't help but put myself in the kids' shoes. If they grow up too sheltered or controlled, or if they see adults fighting because of their food allergies, I fear for the long-term emotional effects. Maybe they'll never feel comfortable living on their own. Maybe they'll isolate themselves. Maybe they'll feel trapped and have an emotional breakdown years down the road.

Parents and guardians of kids with food allergies: I have no idea how to be a parent, and my mom always told me I didn't come with an instruction manual. All I can offer is the perspective of a grown-up kid with food allergies, so here's my recommendation.

If you have a child, try to be conscious of how they may be perceiving your actions, and consider the ripple effects. If you have a teenager or young adult, try to understand that your kid is not a child anymore, and they do go to great lengths to keep themselves safe when not under your nose.

If you're picking up on any snide comments or sense your kid is pushing the limits with what they know they cannot eat, they may be trying to tell you what they need, but just don't know how to bring it up. Come from a place of love and have an open conversation.

My recommendation for any young adult with food allergies: Communicate with your loved ones early on. Write your thoughts down first and bring notes so you don't forget anything in the heat of the moment. Be true to what you need, but also try to remember that our parents and loved ones went through hell and back to keep us safe, so we need to meet them in the middle.

Bottom line: I always felt like I needed to over-communicate my food allergies with complete strangers, like restaurant staff, but I ended up neglecting the importance of communicating with those closest to me. Don't make my mistake.

6
Managing Food Allergies in the Office

The working world. It's where you get the opportunity to take on new challenges, flex and grow your skills, be taken seriously—that is, until your department head asks you to join her for lunch.

Let me back up.

Food allergies are seen in society as a sign of weakness or awkwardness. Think about all the times food allergies are portrayed in pop culture. Do you picture a geek? Or Will Smith in *Hitch* chugging Benadryl® trying to salvage his date? Or Charlie Day repeatedly stabbing Kevin Spacey in the chest and neck with an auto-injector in *Horrible Bosses*? (By the way, that's not how it works. An epinephrine auto-injector should be administered via the thigh for three to ten seconds, depending on the brand. Always carefully read the instructions.)

You may have seen or heard about the viral Tweet in March 2019, with nearly two hundred thousand likes and nearly sixty thousand retweets, which read, "Unpopular opinion; Coraline is one of the best movies ever and the people who are scared of it are the people allergic to peanuts, weak ass kids."[3]

If I wanted to be taken seriously as a woman in corporate America, in the financial services industry, my food allergies were the last thing I wanted to disclose.

In fact, anyone who's applied for a job recently may remember a section of the application with the opportunity to disclose a disability. The ADA requires employers to make reasonable accommodations for employees or candidates with

---

[3] This Tweet has been deleted. I was able to find it by searching the internet, though I don't recommend digging up this type of content, unless you're prepared to go down that rabbit hole.

disabilities, but does not require candidates to disclose disabilities to employers or potential employers.

I struggle with this. If I do *not* disclose, an employer is not legally required to make accommodations should I ever need them.

But if I *do* disclose, I can't shake this scenario from my head: A human resources rep asks me about my disability, and when I say I have food allergies, they try to hide a smirk and say, "Oh, I thought you meant a *real* disability."

On previous job applications, I always declined this section. But, when filling out my most recent application, I thought back to my very first job after college.

I was a travel writer for a small travel and group tourism magazine. My boss wanted me to do a highway spotlight on a dairy farm in Indiana. I reminded him that I may not be the best person for this assignment as I wouldn't be able to exactly immerse myself into the whole experience.

When he told me I'd be fine, I joked that I couldn't write the story if I ended up hospitalized and on workers' comp. I still went on the road trip, but a coworker came with me to experience the food and cow-milking and cheese-making activities, while I fed a goat on the other side of the farm.

In an alternate universe, had I been told to go alone, I would have no legal ground to stand on if I refused and got fired. So, I decided to disclose my food allergies, but I still try to avoid bringing attention to them at work.

Not only is it hard for me to feel I can be taken seriously with my food allergies lingering in the background, but my allergies actually impact work activities. If you work in an office setting or similar, think about how many times someone brings donuts, or when your boss takes the team out to lunch, or when you get a cupcake for your birthday. People gather, eat, and make small talk. With me, it's usually about my allergies and why I'm not eating. I've even purposefully not attended a work breakfast or two because I knew all that my coworkers would talk to me about is why I'm not eating or why I'm only eating fruit, followed by a list of questions I've answered millions of times before. Not an efficient use of my time.

And let's not forget about team volunteer activities that involve preparing meals. When I'm the only one who doesn't jump to clean tables, or when I say the only job I can do is cut vegetables or put away clean dishes, I can't help but feel lazy—and laziness is the last trait I want to portray to my colleagues.

In each of these situations, people with food allergies need to adapt. Maybe they'll politely decline a donut and say they've already eaten. Maybe they'll wait to eat their packed lunch when they return from the restaurant. Or, maybe they'll just shut up and graciously accept the vegan cupcake their boss went out of his way to buy but they didn't trust it so they discreetly put it in their backpack to take home to their spouse. (That last one was oddly specific, wasn't it?)

All of that said, I do leverage my food-sharing, friend-making tactic in the office to build relationships with colleagues. If the company hands out treats for a business anniversary, I'll give mine to a coworker instead. If a vendor sends a box of chocolates, I'll set them out on the community table for all to enjoy.

I encourage anyone with food allergies to strike a balance when it comes to talking about your food allergies at work. I wouldn't go in on your first day and make a big deal about your restricted diet, potentially branding yourself as the food allergy person, but don't completely avoid the topic or isolate yourself. If you're at a team lunch waiting for food, don't complain that you can't eat or that you're starving, but if someone asks about it, turn it into a conversation topic.

Allowing room for a little humor has always helped me.

I remember once I was preparing for a weekend trip to Milwaukee with a few work friends. We planned on leaving straight from work, so I bought a loaf of bread and a jar of peanut butter to prepare my sandwiches for the weekend.

I booked a conference room, placed my laptop to my left and my food supplies to my right, and made peanut butter sandwiches while keeping an eye on my email. What's the worst that could happen? I'll tell you: The senior vice president of corporate communications walked in and saw me making peanut butter sandwiches in the conference room—not exactly what this room is intended for. I, holding a knife in one hand and a slice of bread in the other, slowly turned to face her.

"It's for Milwaukee!" I exclaimed.

(I'm so awkward. She had no idea, to my knowledge, about the weekend getaway.)

As I was about to elaborate, she doubled over with laughter. For my next few years at the company, it came up as a funny memory, and on my last day before venturing for my new job, my parting gift was a box of Jif To Go® peanut butter cups.

When I started my new job, I received a calendar invite to have lunch with the head of my department, the chief marketing officer (CMO). I didn't feel it was appropriate to ask my boss's boss if she wouldn't mind grabbing coffee, instead. She didn't yet know about my food allergies, and I didn't want to come across as inflexible or demanding as a new employee.

When we sat down at the restaurant and the server took our order, I asked for a plain salad—literally just greens and tomatoes, with no dressing—and when I explained it was due to food allergies, I could feel the server's annoyance. After she begrudgingly took our orders, the CMO didn't dote on my food allergies before we dove into talking about work. I was relieved.

When I received my salad, I remember thinking things were going so well. I took a tiny bite, as is my tradition. The CMO asked me about social media employee advocacy when my tongue began to itch.

"When it comes to getting employees engaged on social media, we'll want to first…"

While talking, I was opening a Benadryl® under the table and paused to pop it in my mouth and take a swig of water. I was so sneaky.

"…consider the business goals—"

"Did you just take a Benadryl®? Are you okay?" the CMO asked.

Busted.

I told her my tongue started to itch, so I figured I'd take a Benadryl® to stay on the safe side. I assured her I packed a lunch that day, just in case, and I could easily wait until I got back to my desk to eat. We moved on with talking about work. She didn't make me feel an ounce of discomfort or guilt as she proceeded to eat her lunch while I talked away about social media best practices in support of business goals.

When the server returned to check on us, she noticed I had barely touched my salad. The CMO told her I had a reaction, and I internally chuckled at how quickly her mood flipped from annoyed to genuinely concerned. I told her it was fine and asked for the salad to be boxed so I could take it home to my husband.

Despite the lunch not exactly going the way I planned, I walked away feeling more comfortable around my new grand boss and, to put in corporate tone, to feel free to bring my true and authentic self to the workplace. Plus, it doesn't hurt knowing a leader can back me up in case anyone questions the severity of my food allergies.

Food allergies don't just impact interactions with colleagues and internal company activities. Having meals with external parties (i.e., clients, vendors) is an extremely practical and traditional way of meeting at just the right level of formality. People with food allergies can't exactly do that. Imagine trying to close a deal then having to excuse yourself to take anti-histamines after one bite of your lunch, to be followed by thirty or so minutes of your prospective client feeling uncomfortable as you stare at them while they eat. Whenever I meet with clients and vendors, I ask to meet at a coffee shop or invite them to my office for a tour of the building, instead.

A word of caution on meeting in coffee shops: Airborne allergens can cause reactions. More than once I've needed to excuse myself from an enclosed coffee shop to step outside and pop some Benadryl®. I believe the blame is on steamed milk and/or roasted nuts.

This brings me to the work environment itself, as well as the commute.

Whenever I get situated in a new work environment, I mentally note convenience stores nearby or on my way to the office where I can buy food and snacks.

Sometimes, I don't have time (or I completely forget) to make breakfast or pack my lunch.

I once purchased pre-packaged cereal and a banana from a sundry shop, and as I was checking out, the cashier told me I should buy some milk with my cereal.

"No, thanks," I said with a smile.

He replied, "No, really, it's small and perfect on the go."

I was in a hurry, so to shut down the conversation, I handed him my credit card and said, "Oh, no, I'm allergic to milk, but thanks!"

I shit you not, he replied, "Allergic? No, don't do that. Milk is good for you!"

I will say this for a life with food allergies: There's never a dull moment!

Take this story, for instance. On the first day of a previous job, after I sat down at my new desk and began typing, my wrists began to itch. I'm assuming there was something left behind on the desk or keyboard from whoever occupied the desk before me. I experience similar situations when I eat my lunch in the cafeteria. The messes adults leave behind never cease to amaze me.

Can we all just promise right now to clean up after ourselves when we leave a shared space? And I'm not just talking about café tables.

One morning, I was on the train on my way to work, and the skin under my knees and thighs started itching and burning. I was wearing a high-waisted business skirt that unfortunately hiked up a bit when I sat down. I stood up and turned to look at my hamstrings, then at the seat.

There was tan dust stuck to my legs and spread across the seat. I looked at the floor and saw a cashew and a pistachio. I sat on nut dust. For shit's sake. That's what I get for looking at my phone while sitting down. I had another thirty minutes or so before we got to my stop, so I picked up my bag and went to the train car's bathroom.

I ran a paper towel under cold water and went to find a different, clean seat. The cool cloth soothed my legs, and the itching was gone by the time I got off the train, but I still made a pit stop to buy antihistamine cream, which I keep in my commuter bag at all times.

When I got to the office, my work friend asked me why the bottom of my skirt was damp. The wet cloth. I hurried to the bathroom to put my ass up to the hand dryer.

Despite any food-allergy-induced embarrassment at work, I love my job. I often give presentations on various social media topics to varying audiences, but I always close the same way. Allow me to put on my corporate hat and provide three key takeaways and next steps for each of my target audiences before I close this chapter.

If you have food allergies:

1. Put yourself into a position where you will be most comfortable and confident. While work inherently calls for you to go out of your comfort zone every now and then, you can control your confidence. For example, I tend to use humor when talking about my food allergies to ease my nerves, but this can backfire in the workplace. I have over-used humor by poking fun at myself, but this damaged my credibility. So, I fuel my confidence in other ways during those important meetings and presentations, such as making small talk beforehand or memorizing a few powerful statistics to establish my expertise.

2. Have an open dialogue with key players at work. This could be someone in human resources, your boss, a coworker, clients—anyone whose knowledge of your food allergies would make both your lives easier.

3. Plan, then plan on not having a plan. You may think you've prepared all your meals for the workday, until you get a last-minute invite to a work-related happy hour or charity event. Keep non-perishable, easily transportable snacks in your bag or at your desk.

If you don't have food allergies and have a colleague or direct report who does:

1. People with food allergies are not defined by their allergies, so try to find different things to make small talk about during work gatherings where food is involved.

2. If your team is planning an outing that involves eating or preparing food, speak up. Ask the person with food allergies what they're comfortable with, or, if you can help it, avoid food-focused activities altogether.

3. Remember, people with food allergies tend to be adaptable and detail-oriented, which double as positive qualities on a résumé!

That's all the time we have for today, folks. Thank you for your attention. Warm regards.

7
A Milk-Free Sex Life

No Whipped Cream in the Bedroom

My eighth-grade Halloween party was over and I stood in my parents' front yard. The moon had just reappeared from behind dark clouds, illuminating his brown eyes looking into mine. Through my sandals, I could feel the wet, cold grass brush against my bare toes.

His friends called for him in the distance, but our eyes remained locked. His friends yelled again, closer this time, which broke my gaze. The next thing I knew, my cheek was in his palm and his lips locked with mine. I had to stand on my tippy toes to keep my lips pressed to his. My calves stretched, but I dared not break this dreamy kiss.

When he pulled away, he smiled at me, then ran toward his friends' echoes. I remained standing, nay, floating, toes beginning to numb. I didn't care. I could still feel his lips on mine. I could feel…oh shit.

My fairy-tale moment was cockblocked by an allergic reaction.

My lips itched and swelled. *Now* my pre-teen brain could recall him arriving at my parents' house with a milkshake.

Great, now I had to go back into my house, cover my lips and stealthily grab Benadryl® and ice—all without my parents noticing. I wasn't about to explain to my dad, who to this day I'm positive believes I haven't the slightest clue what a penis is, that I kissed a boy and was now having an allergic reaction. I sprawled face down on my bed, firmly pressing the ice to my lips, praying my parents didn't knock on my bedroom door just yet to ask how the party went.

I couldn't get the story my mom had told me just weeks before out of my mind: A girl from Canada who was severely allergic to peanuts died of an anaphylactic shock after kissing a boy at a party who ate peanuts. I took a series of deep breaths to see if my breathing changed. The itching stopped, and I showed no other signs of an allergic reaction. I was in the clear. No kiss of death tonight.

From then on, I was careful and communicative when it came to locking lips. I'd be upfront about my allergies and avoid kisses that could kill. This didn't always work out in my favor.

Do you know how hard it is to ask someone to wash their mouth in a sexy way right before making out? In the most intimate moment, right before the kiss, the point of no return—I chose that as my opportune moment to warn them about their contaminated lips.

But, which is worse? Waiting to see if a guy even wants to kiss me until I tell him, or tell him in advance and come across as overly confident?

I've tried both, and unfortunately most guys would run the other way after I dropped this bomb, "Hey, if you're planning on kissing me tonight, don't eat that cheeseburger."

All of this became easier as I got older and dating became more formal. I went from sneaking kisses in the dark to planning actual dates. A boy would ask if I wanted to grab dinner and a movie. This was my chance to tell him up front that I couldn't do dinner because I have life-threatening food allergies, and my doctor told me to never eat out, and he also warned me about kissing someone who just had milk or nuts (which was a lie, but it fit into this conversation better than in the heat of the moment).

Turning twenty-one opened a new door: going out for drinks. I was able to eat dinner at home first, then meet at a bar for a pre-movie adult beverage. I had to feel out when it was a good time to tell my date about my food allergies. Sometimes I would tell him after a few initial conversations; other times I would wait until we were actually at the bar when he asked if I wanted an appetizer. When I was on dating apps, I disclosed my food allergies in my bio and weeded out anyone who saw that as a deal breaker.

Each boy reacted differently when I told him about my food allergies. Some would get excited about a cheap date, some would become genuinely interested, and some practically ignored my disability.

One boy in particular lasted a few months, until he took me to Chicago to a few of his favorite bars. He wouldn't shut up about how he's tight with all the coolest bartenders. I suppose he wasn't lying—one bartender gave us shots on the house. He wouldn't say what they were, but I knew as soon as he set them down that I'd have to pass.

It was a dark liquor. I tend to steer clear of dark liquor because some contain caramel for color. I told the boy I wasn't comfortable taking it and offered it to him.

"I don't want it," he replied.

"Okay, what should I do?" I asked.

"I don't know."

I asked the couple next to us if they wanted it. They declined.

I didn't want the bartender to think I didn't take his shot, and it's not like either of us had the time or patience for me to explain why, so I quickly dumped the shot into the drain in front of us.

The boy acted like I just shot the bartender in cold blood.

"*Why* would you do that? That's my *boy*! You better hope he didn't *see* that. He's *never* going to give me a free shot again. Thanks a lot. This is so *embarrassing*," he cringed.

I broke up with him shortly after. This brings me to the winner.

I met my husband in the vegan- and gluten-free aisle of a grocery store on April 6, 2015. He asked what I was shopping for. I told him I was buying chocolate, then, in an extremely smooth manner, I felt the need to quickly explain why I was spending above average for a chocolate bar.

"I have food allergies!" I practically yelled it.

I calmed myself and continued to explain this was the only nearby place that sold chocolate I could eat. We talked for about twenty minutes as shoppers weaved around us. For the first time, I wasn't annoyed at the grocery store (but more on that in chapter nine).

He then offered to continue our conversation over a beer at the bar next door. This man wasn't intimidated by my allergies. He could have politely told me to enjoy my shopping and never spoken to me again. But, he wanted to learn more about me as a whole. He told me my food allergies are a part of me, and he wanted to get to know the other parts. I was smitten.

On one of our first dates, he offered to make us dinner at his house, with my supervision, so I could make sure all the ingredients and utensils were okay.

If you don't have food allergies and are interested in making a special meal for a special someone, I have a few tips.

You can do what my husband did and embed the act of cooking into the date itself.

Alternatively, if you're making the dinner on your own, be sure to check every single ingredient, even if you think there's zero chance of the allergen being present. Text pictures of the ingredients to your special someone, not just for safety, but also to reassure them—dating is nerve-wracking enough!

If texting isn't an option, keep all the original packaging so they can read the ingredients before you're ready to eat. It may sound over the top, but gestures like that go a long way in easing the vibe and avoiding any mood-killing moments.

If you have food allergies and are single and ready to mingle, I'm going to give you two bites of advice that I learned from my dating days:

1. If you're ever with someone who makes you feel even remotely ashamed for having food allergies, walk away. I've been with the guy who rushed me to eat so we can meet his friends for dinner (where I would sit and watch them eat), the guy who spoke for me when I was asked about my allergies, and the guy who jokingly held cheese above my head. Thank you, next.

2. Put yourself into a situation where you will be most comfortable and confident. I know I said this before, but I can't stress it enough. If you're comfortable, you're being your true self. If you're confident, well, that's just sexy!

So, there's what I can share on dating with food allergies.

You're probably thinking, *When is this girl going to get to the part about sex?*

Not to sound anti-climactic, but once you've mastered the art of telling someone to brush their teeth before kissing you and not killing the mood, it really isn't all that different from normal sex. Of course, there are limitations and precautions.

If you have food allergies, imagine your special someone just ate something you're allergic to, then immediately brushed their teeth. Even though they brushed, this tactic is not guaranteed to prevent a reaction. Maybe you'd be comfortable kissing, but I'm willing to bet you'd prefer if their mouth didn't go near a more intimate, sensitive place (if you know what I mean).

If you're interested in incorporating food into your sex life, and either you or your partner has food allergies, may I suggest a few alternatives? I've found chocolate syrup typically does not contain any major allergens in its ingredients. Fruit is usually a safe option, too (unless of course the allergy is to that fruit). I have yet to find totally dairy-free whipped cream. Plenty of brands claim to be dairy-free, but look closely at the ingredients; they can include whey and casein, which are byproducts of milk.

As a rule to live by, always ask and always first check ingredients; it applies to everyday meals *and* sex!

If you're worried about what your sex partner may think or say, I asked my husband if he thinks my allergies have affected our sex life in any way.

"I just need to be conscious of what I eat. When you come home from work and try to give me a kiss, you have no idea what I recently ate, so that becomes my responsibility," he said. "But your food allergies don't affect our sex life other than the kissing part...and the fact that you can never have a banana split."

A banana split is apparently something involving ice cream, whipped cream, chocolate, a cherry, and...you know what...the banana part goes without saying.

My point is: Have an open dialogue with your partner about what you're comfortable with as well as what they're comfortable with. It's a lot easier to laugh off an awkward conversation than to have your night end with a trip to the hospital instead of an orgasm.

8
Wedding Planning

To Have and to Hold My EpiPen®

I'd come a long way from warning boys about kissing me after they ate a cheeseburger. My husband proposed during the August 2017 eclipse while we were visiting Mt. Hood, Oregon. I was on cloud nine. I was engaged! I was about to make plans for the big day where I'd promise my unconditional love to my best friend forever. I was—oh crap, about to plan a wedding.

If you've ever planned or helped plan a wedding, you know it is not an easy feat. Imagine planning a wedding with the added bonus of a life-threatening food allergy. Hiding in my room after getting puffy lips from a kiss in junior high is one thing, but what if I had a reaction in front of all my family, in-laws and friends?

Much of my wedding planning was done on the fly, and I learned along the way. With the hopes of helping betrothed readers prep for their nuptials, I've highlighted the five main elements that were impacted by my food allergies when planning my wedding, and how I made each work for my big day.

The Venue

One of the things I did not realize was that venues often have limitations when it comes to caterers. I have a married friend who knew exactly who she wanted to do their cake, only to find out that their venue only allowed for certain bakeries. As you can imagine, this would be problematic for people with food allergies who are only able to choose from select caterers and bakers to begin with. To avoid being pigeonholed, I recommend first finding a venue with flexible catering options and locking down your date with that venue.

You may also want to consider how comfortable you are with the venue being a certain distance from the nearest medical center. If you were to have a reaction on your big day that required medical attention, would you be comfortable at a barn fifty miles from the nearest hospital?

I cannot stress this enough: Be very transparent with the venue staff about your food allergies. The more the wedding-day venue coordinator knows, the more prepared they will be should the worst happen.

Makeup

"I'm at Sephora and the makeup artist asked this woman if she was allergic to anything and she said 'shrimp,'" read the Tweet of comedian Sam Reece in January 2019.

Turns out, according to allergy-insight.com, *chitosan* is a cosmetic ingredient derived from the shells of crustaceans. A tip of the hat to that Sephora employee for asking about allergies. Moral of the story? Never bury the lede. When I was the matron of honor for Mollie (remember Mollie, who unintentionally spilled the Boston beans?), I told the makeup artist about my allergies before I sat down.

"Milk, you said? Okay…I'm just going to put this liquid foundation way over here, far, *far* away from you," she said as she reached for a new, clean brush.

Crisis averted.

Before booking a makeup artist, ask if they can work with products that are safe for you. It could not only save your life, but also save you any non-refundable deposits.

The Dress

A food allergy impacting makeup options may not surprise you, but what does a dress have to do with anything?

One word: pockets. You can keep your medication on you at all times. You can either buy a dress with pockets, or most tailors and seamstresses can add pockets.

If you're going for a dress that's more fitting, skip the pockets turn a garter into a holster for your auto-injector. You can find garters that are meant to store flasks online; just swap the flask for your auto-injector and you're good to go!

For those of you planning on wearing a suit to your wedding, I'd actually recommend against pockets if the outline of your belongings (phone, auto-injector) will show in pictures, or if you want to avoid being asked, "Is that an epinephrine auto-injector in your pocket, or are you just happy to see me?"

I must admit that I did not have pockets or a garter, and that I entrusted my husband and parents to carry my medicine for me. Looking back, it did cause me a little stress not having my auto-injector on me at all times; every other day of every other year I've always carried it. I felt naked, like how you'd feel if you forgot your phone at home—except your life depended on it. Wherever you keep your auto-injector on your big day, make sure you have more than one and know where they are at all times.

Wedding Invites

On our wedding invitations, we added a line asking the open-ended question, "Do you have any dietary restrictions?"

I would have felt hypocritical if I didn't at least attempt to make accommodations.

This open-ended question worked for us because we didn't make any promises while showing we were still potentially able to meet guests' needs. When we received the RSVPs, we texted those who indicated they had dietary restrictions to ask them if they'd be comfortable picking and choosing from the buffet, or if they'd prefer to order the eggplant as a separate dish served directly to them by the caterer.

Catering & The Cake

I was fully prepared to eat a turkey sandwich at my wedding instead of risk becoming a headline where the bride died due to an allergic reaction. All eyes would be on me, and I was not willing to risk it. My family urged me to at least discuss my food allergies with caterers and feel it out. They spent their lives watching me eat cold turkey sandwiches at countless dinner tables and wanted to see me eat a proper meal on my wedding day. I agreed to at least try.

We shopped around a bit to compare which venues allowed for what caterers. I won't lie, it was like being a project manager, on top of my full-time job, to balance phone calls with caterers, interviewing them on their abilities to accommodate for food allergies, and phone calls with venues, asking if they recommend any caterers who have dealt with food allergies in the past. I made a spreadsheet (to no one's surprise).

But by this point in my life, I learned to pinpoint the difference between restaurant managers feigning accommodations for a dollar and those who actually cared for my well-being, even if it meant losing a sale. I found these positive characteristics in a local restaurant and in my bridesmaid's mom.

We catered with a local barbecue joint. I explained my food allergies to the restaurant manager, and the team went above and beyond to accommodate my big day.

They explained which menu options I could not eat due to ingredients and cross-contamination, which options I could safely eat, and what cooking surfaces were only used for those options. That's how we narrowed down the wedding menu.

I did actually want some non-Lauren-friendly buffet items available for guests—half of my in-laws live in Wisconsin; could you imagine if I didn't offer anything covered in cheese? It just had to be at the far end of the buffet table. The table also included labels for dairy-free and gluten-free options, per our guests' previously noted dietary restrictions.

When it came time for the tasting, we sat down as a family in the restaurant and they made us feel like royalty. I was eating much slower than my husband and in-laws, as I was taking small bites and waiting, but we were halfway through the menu and I had no reactions.

Then I tried a bite of the broccoli salad, and my tongue began to itch. The server had made himself so available and welcoming that I felt comfortable immediately asking him about the dressing. It was Italian. Typically, Italian dressing contains no milk or milk products, but he beelined to the kitchen to check the ingredients. Whey was one of the ingredients in the dressing. He and the manager apologized profusely. To ensure this didn't happen again on my big day, the catering staff made my entire plate separately, first, and delivered it to me straight from the kitchen.

A lot of people say they've dreamed about their wedding day ever since they were a little kid. I dreamed of my wedding cake. It would be milk- and nut-free, and it would be a yellow cake with white icing—a lot of icing. I lucked out in that the mother of one of my bridesmaids, Dede, is actually a professional chef and baker.[4] She agreed to not only bake our personal wedding cake, but also to make desserts for all of our guests.

Dede, with help from my bridesmaids and their families, put together a tasting for me, my husband and my parents.

Lemon mousse. Raspberry pastry cream. Dairy-free cupcakes with dairy-free icing made with coconut cream. (My tree-nut allergy does not include coconut.) There was no way I'd be able to get through this without a reaction. Nothing that looked or smelled this good could possibly be completely free of milk or nuts. Upon seeing the spread, I secretly developed a sneaky plan to take Benadryl® in the bathroom. Everyone worked so hard, and the presentation was so perfect; I couldn't bear to have a reaction in front of them.

---

[4] Dede McAllen Dezelski has graciously offered for anyone to reach out to her with further questions at dedesews2@aol.com.

But, I tried every dessert at the tasting with no reactions, and my husband and I picked the top four that Dede would make for the wedding—for two hundred and fifty guests. I'm not sure if it was the sugar rush or the mimosas, but about halfway through tasting the chocolate marshmallow Dede crafted into a cowboy boot for my husband, I started to well up.

Despite all the planning frustrations and roadblocks, this was the point: I was about to marry the man I love, and my family and friends fully supported me. The moments like this remind me that my food allergies do not define me, and if I ever feel alone or misunderstood, I know I have an outstanding support system.

9
Navigating Food Labels
& Ingredients

This Chapter is Gluten Free!

I hate going to the grocery store. People leave their carts in the middle of the aisles. Kids run around and knock things off shelves. Shoppers try to cut you in line. They blatantly lie that they have fifteen items or less in their cart. Grocery shopping is not enjoyable.

Now, throw food allergies into the mix.

Grocers are always trying to push samples on me even after I politely decline. Spending an extra twenty minutes picking up items off the shelf, reading ingredients, and putting them back makes me literally groan out loud, which weirds out other shoppers.

These shoppers simultaneously get annoyed with me when I do this "shelf dance" and take up a side of the aisle they're trying to race down. I was actually once in the checkout line reading the ingredients on a pack of gum (remember my geometry class experience), and, all of a sudden, my cart shook. I looked back and this person hit the back of my cart with the front of her cart. I assumed it was an accident, but this woman stared me in the face and hit my cart again!

Anyway, I think what I hate most about that "shelf dance" is the buildup and disappointment of reading ingredients in the grocery store. Some of this is rooted in trust. For example, I'll purchase the brand of bagels I've eaten for the past few years, then have one for breakfast and get an itchy tongue. I'll check the label to see that they either changed their ingredients or added a disclaimer that says it was manufactured in a facility with milk or tree nuts. But, the big part of that is *how* companies label their products.

Diet fads get in the way of providing factual information. A loaf of bread may say "gluten free" in big bold letters on the front of the package only for someone to closely read the ingredients and see that it was manufactured in the same facility as wheat. I've seen "non-dairy creamer" with whey in the ingredients.

While people with food allergies may be used to reading every single word on every single label, most people don't do this. Why would they? I once had a friend who insisted on baking Lauren-friendly brownies. The chocolate chips she used were vegan, which was displayed loudly across the front of the packaging. However, the chips were manufactured in a facility with milk products. She was so upset with herself, but I did not blame her one bit. I blame these companies' marketing departments (and that's saying something from someone who makes a living off marketing).

When did "gluten free" become the diet trend to be boldly advertised on the front of the box, while other common allergens are printed in tiny font on the back of the box under the nutrition facts and ingredients? Furthermore, these aren't always included on individual packages and are even sometimes covered up with price stickers. I once tried to move the sticker to see the ingredients on a to-go box of cereal, then the convenience store worker asked if I was trying to steal it.

When a brand changes ingredients, I feel disappointed, and maybe even a little betrayed. When they add the "made in a facility with…" disclaimer, I just get mad. It's like, I ate this product last week, but now I can't unsee this warning label, so you're putting the gamble on me. I have enough to worry about.

And *then* there are labels that say, "Manufactured in a facility with milk, but we take precautions to ensure no cross contamination."

So, am I supposed to just trust that? It's all so mentally taxing.

Labels. Can't live with 'em; can't live without 'em. Literally. Here's what happened to me when a brand omitted a key label from their product's packaging.

I purchased a muffin, which I've had plenty of times before over the course of several years. I read the package to ensure there was nothing new and no cross-contamination disclaimer. As you can see in the photo, there was nothing on this package that indicated any presence or potential presence of milk or tree nuts.

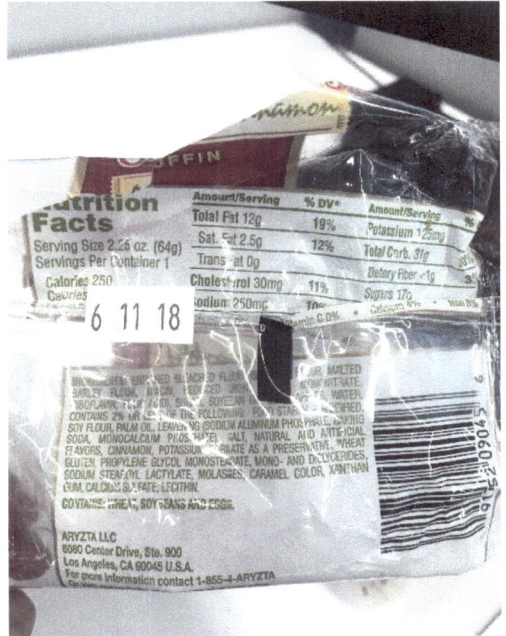

After one bite, my tongue began to itch, my throat felt warm, my heart raced. I scanned the ingredient list again. And again. Did I develop a new food allergy? Do I need to go through more rounds of testing and food journaling and have to take a safety taste before everything I eat now?

I ended up emailing the brand, with a picture of the package, serial number, and location of purchase. They confirmed the muffin was made in a facility with milk and tree nuts.

Thus began a three-month process of educating myself on food label laws. Turns out, that "made in a facility with…" label is not legally required by the U.S. Food and Drug Administration (FDA).

What if a teacher or parent had given a child this muffin, and the kid ate the whole thing? What if someone died because of a lack of communication? I wrote a letter to my local congress member and petitioned the FDA to make a change, but never received a response.

Coming to the food allergy community's rescue, FARE and the Grocery Manufacturers Association announced on August 26, 2019, they will work together to address the need for federal, uniform standards for allergen labeling.

Their press release states, "A national, uniform allergen labeling policy, determined at the federal level, is of critical importance to protecting the public health of the 32 million Americans with food allergies."

I'm grateful for efforts like this to help make the world that much more safe for people with food allergies. Despite obstacles and challenges and irritating trips to the grocery store, I'm hopeful for the future.

10
Foretelling a Future with Food Allergies

What a time to be alive in the food allergy community.

In September 2016, the U.S. House Committee on Oversight and Government Reform called Heather Bresch, CEO of Mylan—the pharmaceutical company that manufactures the EpiPen®—to testify amidst public outrage over the high cost of an EpiPen® two-pack. The list price had risen to $600 for a pair of the auto-injectors, compared to $100 in 2007.

Mylan began offering a generic version of the EpiPen® in 2016, and, in August 2018, the FDA approved the first generic version of Mylan's EpiPen® to be manufactured by an outside competitor, Teva Pharmaceutical Industries.

Just when I felt I could finally get this life-saving drug and not break the bank, in 2018, the food allergy community was faced with one of our worst nightmares—a shortage of epinephrine auto-injectors.

This shortage lasted through June 2019, according to FARE, due to "manufacturing delays." (I recall it took me about a week, after my auto-injector was already expired, to get my prescription filled.) In response to this national shortage, the FDA extended the expiration dates for specific lots of EpiPen® and the authorized generic auto-injectors.

After wandering through a dark, decade-long tunnel, lined with price tags and question marks regarding the rest of my life with food allergies, I'm starting to see the light.

There are new breakthroughs in research for a cure and treatment options. Oral immunotherapy (OIT), for example, is an approximately year-long treatment with the goal of re-training the immune system to tolerate allergens through a steady increase of tiny amounts. I've been on an OIT waiting list for over a year for my milk allergy; only two doctors in the state of Illinois offer the treatment (as of April 2019).

While OIT is not currently FDA approved, in September 2019, the FDA voted seven to two to approve Palforzia, the "peanut pill," to help reduce allergic reactions for patients ages four to seventeen as part of OIT protocol.

In April 2019, I attended the FARE Chicago Spring Luncheon, where I heard from some of the most brilliant minds on the front lines of food allergy breakthroughs. Dr. Cathryn Nagler, the Bunning Food Allergy Professor and Professor of Pathology, Medicine, Pediatrics and The College at the University of Chicago, is examining how—prepare yourself—commensal bacteria regulate susceptibility to allergic responses to food (I pulled this from the luncheon's program).

Dr. Nagler discussed how (and now I'm paraphrasing) the cause of food allergies can't be genetic alone because of the rapid increase of food allergies across generations—it has to be related to our environment. She went on to explain how we've lost essential bacteria, and a synthetic form of bacteria metabolite could restore that lost bacteria. I also read in the program that Dr. Nagler has applied insights from studying pre-clinical gnotobiotic murine models of cow's milk allergy to launch a new company, ClostraBio, which is developing microbiome-modulating therapeutics for the prevention and treatment of food allergies.

In June 2019, Boston Magazine published an article featuring research from Brigham and Women's and Boston Children's Hospital suggesting that certain gut bacteria may prevent—and even reverse—food allergies.

When I learn about all these efforts and findings, I can't help but feel hopeful for the food allergy community's future.

When it comes to foretelling *my* future with food allergies, I remain cautiously optimistic.

My husband and I want to have kids. I've read countless contradictory articles on whether or not consuming an allergen during pregnancy increases or decreases a baby's chance of developing food allergies, the role breastfeeding plays, or how a kid's diet can or cannot lead to food allergies.

If my kids do end up with food allergies, I will at least be able to apply my experiences, but I know they will have a very different upbringing than I did decades before them. Sure, I'm confident I'll be able to plan a family vacation, but will I unintentionally emotionally damage my kids?

I wonder if it's even possible to raise a child with food allergies and ensure they grow up without any emotional baggage.

Food Allergy & Anaphylaxis Connection Team (FAACT) has a tab on its website, *Psychological Impact*, which contains various findings on the topic. Below are findings from surveys of parents or caregivers of children with food allergies:

- 59% reported school field trips were affected by food allergies
- 58% thought that food allergy affected their child's 'playing at friends' house'
- 50% or more survey respondents indicated that food allergies significantly affected their family social activities
- 41% reported a significant impact on their stress levels
- 34% reported that food allergy had an impact on the child's school attendance
- 10% choose to home-school their children because of food allergies

FAACT also reports this finding from the study, *The Impact of Food Allergy on the Daily Activities of Children and Their Families*, "Children with more than two food allergies and their parents report poor quality of life."

When children are reporting a poor quality of life, you know something needs to change.

When I read these findings, I have flashbacks: a classmate's mom (a complete stranger) carrying my EpiPen® for me on a field trip because I wasn't trusted with it; wearing a laminated string necklace to school events telling others not to feed me; compulsively checking ingredients at least two times; making jokes instead of letting friends and family feel sorry for me.

It's no wonder I was diagnosed with obsessive-compulsive disorder and anxiety when I was in seventh grade. And clearly, I'm not the only one who has been psychologically impacted by the existence of food allergies.

While some of these psychological impacts may just be inherent to having food allergies, I believe improvements can be made from a social standpoint. When my food allergies come up in conversation, there's always that one person who just doesn't respond well.

For example, I've been told, "Lauren, don't eat the potatoes, unless you want to die!"

Call me sensitive, but jokes about me dying from suffocation will never be funny. If you have to make food allergy jokes, put some effort into it.

"Lauren, don't touch the potatoes, unless you want to be like the convict who had food allergies—he broke out!" Now *this* would make me laugh.

An example of a less hurtful, but still disconcerting, response is, "So you can't have milk…does that include cheese?"

It's not necessarily their fault they don't understand basic agriculture. A survey from the Innovation Center for U.S. Dairy found that 48% of American adults don't know where chocolate milk comes from, and 7% think it comes from brown cows.

Here's another example: Someone once asked me if the reason I am so short is due to the fact that I couldn't drink milk when my bones were growing. Those *Got Milk?*® commercials must have really got through to this person. But, no; I can attribute my height to my five-foot-nothing mother.

There have also been responses that are just plain ignorant:

"Are you sure you're not just lactose intolerant?"

"I'd kill myself if I couldn't have milk. Your life must suck."

"I think you're having an imaginary reaction."

If you don't have food allergies, I thank you for taking the time to read this book. It's the people like you who are in a powerful position to advocate for people with food allergies; similar to a man advocating for gender equality. By simply educating yourself and speaking up, you can help reduce the amount of tasteless jokes and hurtful responses like the ones I mentioned above.

If you do have food allergies, I'd urge you to try to have patience when you encounter these responses. (I know you've experienced similar situations.) This one took me a long time to learn, and I'll admit, I haven't perfected it yet. I try to remember that people aren't coming from a place of hatred, just a lack of understanding.

May I suggest setting some life goals to help you keep things in perspective? Take some of mine, for instance. I dreamed of publishing this book. So, when someone told me my life sucked, it just added fuel to my pages. How can you turn moments like these in your favor?

Another one of my goals is to live to be one hundred—to witness the century that saw the inception of the internet, the evolution of social media, and the rise and (fingers crossed) fall of food allergies. So, if someone wants me to try a bite of food I'm not comfortable eating, I can decline without feeling guilty because I'm keeping my eye on the prize.

You may be a doctor or a scientist working hard to evolve treatments or find a cure for food allergies. You may be a parent trying to make the world safer for your child. You may be a food allergy advocate for a friend or loved one. You may, like me, have food allergies and are just tackling one day at a time.

Whoever you are, I'll leave you with this: If you catch me crying over spilled milk, it's absolutely because I'm worrying over something I cannot change. That doesn't mean I can't live my life to the hakuna matata mantra, with the support of my family and friends. In one way or another, we're all coexisting with food allergies and are in this together.